THE
INTERSPIRITUAL MEDITATION
WORKBOOK & JOURNAL

The

InterSpiritual Meditation
Workbook & Journal

Edward W. Bastian, Ph.D.

Albion
Andalus
Boulder, Colorado
2016

*"The old shall be renewed,
and the new shall be made holy."*
– Rabbi Avraham Yitzhak Kook

Albion-Andalus, Inc.
P. O. Box 19852
Boulder, CO 80308
www.albionandalus.com

Spiritual Styles Mandala is a registered Trade Mark ™ of Edward W. Bastian, Ph.D.
Design and composition by Samantha Krezinski, Albion-Andalus Inc.
Cover design by Sari Wisenthal-Shore, Sari Design
The "Flower of InterSpiritual Meditation" envisioned by Edward W. Bastian and created by Lynda Rae.
Photos of Edward W. Bastian by Charles Abbott and Michael Stinson.

ISBN-13: 978-0692566466 (Albion-Andalus Books)

ISBN-10: 0692566465

To exploring a new paradigm of InterSpirituality.

To discover universal processes of contemplation and meditation

shared by the world's spiritual traditions.

To developing a comprehensive, satisfying, and sustainable process of meditation.

To share non-sectarian practice for contemplative communities of people with diverse practices and perspectives.

To gain the knowledge, skills, and experience

for mentoring individual & group InterSpiritual Meditation sessions.

To creating a personal contemplative practice based on one's own spiritual styles

---

This workbook and journal is designed to be used for guided personal study, contemplative mentoring, retreats and workshops (in person & online) in conjunction with two books:
InterSpiritual Meditation and *Meditations for InterSpiritual Practice*

InterSpiritual Meditation (ISM)

ISM is a contemplative process that can be shared by people from diverse perspectives and traditions. It can be practiced alone and in community with others. It pulls together key elements of contemplation and meditation shared by many traditions. In this process we gather in the language of silence and experience inter-connectedness. Joining in stillness, we don't impose on others our own personal beliefs, rituals, or the names for our absolute truths, deities, or God. We honor and celebrate the wise and compassionate practices of all traditions. We discover a profound unity within our diversity. We flourish in the love, peace, compassion, gratitude, and the strength of our shared wisdom. We are of one heart. Quietly, each in our own way, we join in the following seven stages together. The sound of a bell leads us from one stage to the next.

This workbook and journal is designed to be used for guided personal study, contemplative mentoring, retreats and workshops (in person & online) in conjunction with two books:

InterSpiritual Meditation:
A Seven-Step Process Drawn from the World's Spiritual Traditions

Meditations for InterSpiritual Practice:
A Collection of Practices from the World's Spiritual Traditions

For more information on the Spiritual Paths Foundation's
seminars, online courses and mentor training program, please
visit www.spiritualpaths.net, www.interspiritualmeditation.org,
or email ed@spiritualpaths.net

TABLE OF CONTENTS

PREFACE

DURING THE PAST forty-five years, my inner life has been profoundly shaped by wonderful teachers, colleagues, and students, along with life's many challenges. Because of my deep gratitude, I want to share a meditative practice that emerged from this work. I hope it will inform and benefit your personal abd group practice as well as your interactions with people from the world's marvelous variety of contemplative traditions and belief systems.

My Buddhist formation began in my mid-twenties; when I began learning Tibetan and Sanskrit; and through studying with extraordinary teachers in monastic settings in South Asia and America. The fruits of this training ripened in wonderful ways during the past fourteen years as I worked closely with over forty Christian, Buddhist, Muslim, Jewish, Hindu, Taoist, and Native American teachers in our Spiritual Paths programs and books.

InterSpiritual Meditation is the result of both my hope for a mature personal contemplative practice, and my hope to formulate a universal practice that can be done in harmony with people of many traditions. Both hopes have been profoundly informed by my collaboration with great meditative practitioners with a variety of spiritual and secular methods.

First, from the perspective of a personal meditation practice, I have learned that each meditator should both study deeply the practice of a single contemplative tradition, and also to take personal responsibility for the method and the outcome of his or her personal practice that might be drawn from the wisdom of multiple traditions; in my case, a practice which is at the same time Buddhist and inclusive of other traditions that deepen and expand my wisdom, compassion and service. While our teachers and colleagues can impart their wisdom and experience, the actual practice of meditation is something we have to engage in alone with their continued blessings. Working alone, with occasional guidance from our teachers and Mentors and support of our community, we must learn to cultivate the internal processes of our minds, accentuating the positive and eliminating the negative. This work is invisible to the outside world. It is subtle and refined. Like many of life's most precious skills, it takes years to cultivate. Meditation is both an art and a science. It is a cultivated taste. Therefore in the kitchen or laboratory of our minds we must personally apply the science, the recipes, insights, methods, skills, patience, and perseverance we have learned from others.

Second, through many sessions of group meditation with teachers of diverse practices, I have experienced the presence of shared consciousness even though we are all doing different internal practices. In spite of, or perhaps because of our diverse practices, I have found that we actually co-create an InterSpiritual consciousness that is greater than the sum of its parts. This shared experience, I believe, can be a foundation for peace among peoples of all spiritual and non-spiritual beliefs. In this experience we know for certain that we can no longer look at each other as the "other." We become inextricably linked, such that to harm another is to harm our self, and to harm our self is to harm others.

During the past few years I have taught many courses and completed two books on InterSpiritual Meditation and the Mandala Process. However, I realized that I needed to do something more to help people engage in this practice. Therefore, I have compiled this workbook and journal. It is a work in progress that is meant to be used along side the books, the classes, courses, individual mentoring, and workshops. I hope it will help you develop and refine your own meditative practice, and to work in contemplative alliance with others whose inspiration and practices emerge from the world's marvelous variety of beliefs, practices, and traditions.

If you are interested in learning more about retreats, online courses and our mentor training program, please contact me at this email address: ed@spiritualpaths.net

INTRODUCTION

THE WORLD'S RELIGIONS AND INDIGENOUS TRADITIONS have developed many types of contemplation and meditation, each formulated for specific spiritual purposes and specific types of practitioners. InterSpiritual Meditation is neither a replacement nor a synthesis of these. Rather it provides a process drawn from many spiritual and secular resources that can help individuals develop a practice that is at once personal and inclusive. Therefore it also lends itself for use by groups of people from diverse traditions and with diverse individual practices. The following verse by Rumi helps illustrate this possibility:

> If ten lamps are present in one place,
> each differs in form from another;
> yet you can't distinguish whose radiance is whose
> when you focus on the light.
> In the field of spirit there is no division;
> no individuals exist.
> Sweet is the oneness of the Friend with His friends.
> Catch hold of spirit.
> Help this headstrong self disintegrate;
> that beneath it you may discover unity,
> like a buried treasure.
>
> — *Mathnawi I, 678-83* of Jalaluddin Rumi[1]

Because InterSpiritual Meditation is a process and not a one-size-fits-all conclusion, it can provide you with a foundation for a life-long contemplative practice. Life-long, because (a) each step in the process leads us into deeper and deeper realms of discovery and realization, and (b) our own practice evolves and deepens over the course of our lives. Taken together, all the so-called steps are mutually interdependent and provide a context for spiritual maturation.

---

1 translated by Camille and Kabir Helminski in *Rumi Daylight.*

This workbook and journal are designed to support both in-person and online seminars and workshops in conjunction with two books:

❖ *InterSpiritual Meditation: A Seven-Step Process from the World's Spiritual Traditions*

❖ *Meditations for InterSpiritual Wisdom: Practices and Readings from the World's Spiritual Traditions*

This workbook can also be used in conjunction with my other book and course of study called *Mandala: Creating an Authentic Spiritual Path – An InterSpiritual Process.*. This work is designed to help us to honoring our Archetypal Spiritual Styles, Discern Answers to our Spiritual Questions, and cultivate practices that are compatible with your spiritual predispositions.

Following are the primary goals for this workbook:

o To explore the emerging paradigm of InterSpirituality.

o To discover the processes of contemplation and meditation shared by the world's spiritual traditions.

o To identify and honor a contemplative focus that matches your primary spiritual styles.

o To develop and refine both a personal and group meditation practice that is sustainable, satisfying, and inclusive.

o To gain the knowledge, skills, and experience required to facilitate InterSpiritual Meditation sessions with individuals and groups. (A subsequent mentor training certificate program will help you learn to teach others and to lead InterSpiritual group sessions.)

The organization of this workbook presupposes your commitment for ongoing study, discussion, journaling, contemplation, meditation, and application in everyday life. Its contents include the following:

1. An introduction to familiarize you with the general purposes and goals.

2. Definitions of key terms and concepts relating to InterSpirituality.

3. An overview of the entire seven-step process of InterSpiritual Meditation.

4. Individual sections containing poems and scriptural quotes, as well as questions for each of the seven steps to help your develop and refine your own practice.

5. Guidelines for InterSpiritual group discussions.

My intention is to provide you with a process to engage in the inner art and science of meditation in a way that is compatible with your own life experience, spiritual perspectives, spiritual learning style, questions, chosen tradition, and the teachings and examples of others. It is meant to help you to recognize, cultivate, and utilize the innate (and often ignored) capacities of consciousness that can be your internal allies for profound transformation into a wise, compassionate and peaceful person.

Through a process of systematic journaling and meditation on each of the seven steps, you will forge and

refine a meditation that is at once rooted in your tradition, inclusive of contemplative wisdom of other traditions, and a reflection of the sum total of your spiritual exploration and experience.

With the 7-step flow of ISM, please remember that Steps 1–4 are contemplative and entail deep thinking and reflection. Here, as you focus on each topic, you can bring to mind some of your personal journal summaries. In this way, your evolving journal entries will help provide the content for your contemplation.

In Steps 5–6 you enter into the actual meditation. Here, you begin with mindful breathing to calmly engage your mind in a more single pointed, non-conceptual focus on your chosen object(s) of meditation. This can be the meditation you already practice or one that you create for this particular process. If you don't have a specific meditation practice, the breathing meditations explained in the two books will provide you with a place to begin. Your journaling will also help you to refine the 'objects' and purposes for these steps of meditation.

Finally, in Step 7, you return to the contemplative mode as you formulate the dedication you have developed in your journaling.

The combination of meditation and journaling will deepen and strengthen your capacity to be transformed into your ideal being with the qualities you most want to embody. With each step, your mind will be carefully nurtured and prepared for the next steps. In the end, all the steps are mutually interdependent, helping to support and sustain each other.

However, before we embark on the process of creating our own contemplative and meditative practice, we'll begin by defining our terms and exploring the emerging paradigm of InterSpirituality.

DEFINING KEY TERMS

PLEASE BECOME FAMILIAR with the following terms and the ways they are defined in the context of our work. We will be discussing these in class, online forums, and personal mentoring sessions. Please reflect on these terms and definitions in your journal.

INTERSPIRITUALITY

"Humanity stands at a crossroads between horror and hope. In choosing hope, we must seed a new consciousness, a radically fresh approach to life drawing its inspiration from perennial spiritual and moral insights, intuition and experience. We call this new awareness interspiritual, implying not the homogenization of religion, but the recovering of the shared mystic heart beating in the center of the world's deepest spiritual traditions."
— Attributed to Brother Wayne Teasdale

RELIGION

"Religion I take to be concerned with faith in the claims to salvation of one faith tradition or another, an aspect of which is acceptance of some form of metaphysical or supernatural reality, including perhaps an idea of heaven or nirvana. Connected with this are religious teachings or dogma, ritual, prayer, and so on."
— His Holiness the Dalai Lama, *Ethics for the New Millennium*

SPIRITUALITY

"Spirituality I take to be concerned with those qualities of the human spirit—such as love and compassion, patience, tolerance, forgiveness, contentment, a sense of responsibility, a sense of harmony—which bring happiness to both self and others."
— His Holiness the Dalai Lama, *Ethics for the New Millennium*

Spirituality pertains to the essence, or the spirit of our very existence. It entails an intuitive wisdom and experiential knowledge—*gnosis, sophia, prajna, hokhmah, da'at, hikmah*—that transcends our senses and intellect. It is the natural instinct that draws us to the conscious essence at the core of our being. It is the innate impulse that connects us to a higher power, a universal essence, a divine entity, the primordial state of being, or the Ultimate Reality. It is the instinctive inclination towards wisdom and compassion, to be loving and altruistic. Spirituality gives an ultimate meaning and purpose to human life through which we can evolve to our greatest potential.

INTERFAITH

The terms "Interfaith" and "interreligious" pertain to the impulse to find shared values, principles, and customs among the world's religions, and to work together with tolerance and respect for the common good.

Interfaith programs bring together people of various religions to share their beliefs, ethics, customs, principles, rituals, rites of passage, and holidays. These programs generally focus on the social values and cultural forms of different religions, and avoid metaphysical and institutional differences that lead to conflict.

INTERSPIRITUAL

The term "InterSpiritual" pertains to the contemplative, meditative, and mystical experiences that are the foundation for spiritual practice.

Interspirituality connotes an inclusive state of contemplative consciousness that merges with those spiritual experiences that were the creative force for the major religions. It holds the promise of a genuine *sharing* of our respective spiritual experiences, and a conscious joining at the deepest levels of our being. InterSpirituality represents the next phase of understanding and connectivity between people of different spiritual traditions.

CONTEMPLATION

It may be characterized by deep concentration, as well as profound inner observation, insight, analysis, and non-conceptual intuition; both involving and surpassing the intellect. It is a profoundly reflective state of consciousness that can arise, for example, while sitting in silence, reading, being in nature, or engaging in art or music. Spiritual contemplation can be a quality of consciousness that rests within porous boundaries between non-conceptual meditative absorption, and subsequent conceptualization of transcendent experience. Contemplation is our means of consciously traveling back and forth between the sacred and the profane; the divine and the worldly; the mystical and our ordinary sense of reality.

MEDITATION

Meditation is a technique for attuning consciousness, which—depending on the individual, the technique used, and the spiritual context in which it is done—may lead to altered states of awareness (including profound focus and tranquility), usually considered beneficial or transformative for individuals and groups.

In this specific usage, meditation is an activity that enables human consciousness to fulfill its potential to be tranquil, one-pointed, blissful, non-conceptual, wise, compassionate, intuitive, and unified with the truth of our existence. (This truth, and/or its name, may vary depending on each tradition and each individual.)

PRAYER

Prayer is a powerful psychological tool for setting our purpose and intention, for focusing our energy on an intended result. Whether prayer is directed to a divine being, a higher power, within our self, or into the universe, we are evoking a deep personal wish that is far more profound than the mundane desires that generally run through our minds. Prayer activates the capacity of our consciousness to actualize or manifest our most profound and benevolent aspirations for ourselves and others.

INTERSPIRITUAL MEDITATION (ISM)

InterSpiritual Meditation (ISM) is a universal process drawn from the world's spiritual traditions. It helps individuals to cultivate inner peace, wisdom, and compassion. Its seven-step process enables people of different spiritual practices to create engaged contemplative communities based on empathy, understanding, shared contemplative intentions, and compassionate service for the common good. Each of the seven steps provide containers within which meditators can include the wisdom and methods from one tradition, a variety of traditions, and from their own personal life experience.

SPIRITUAL GENOME

Just as each biological species has its own unique genome that gives it life and vitality, so are the founders' spiritual experiences to the life and vitality of each religious tradition. The job of the contemplative is to re-experience this spiritual original genome in order to breathe life and vitality into each tradition. Without this, traditions die and fossilize. Just so, human spirituality must be revitalized by direct experience.

SPIRITUAL DIVERSITY

Just as biological diversity is required for the health of each individual within each species, so is spiritual diversity required for the spiritual health of the planet. Just as species must rub up against each other to reinvigorate the life forces required for survival, so must religions come into contact to stimulate each to regenerate their essential life force.

BIOLOGICAL AND SPIRITUAL DIVERSITY

InterSpiritual Meditation is *not* a genetic hybrid. It is *not* a new religion. It is a process wherein meditators from each tradition can help each other revitalize the unique spiritual genes required both for spiritual diversity and personal spiritual realization. The vitality, viability, and relevance of all religions, spiritual traditions, and people depend, directly or indirectly, on interaction with each other. Indeed, the survival on the human species may depend on this interdependent interaction with the deepest levels of our inter-being-ness.

OPEN-SOURCE SPIRITUALITY

The term "open-source" comes from the language of computer programmers who share code with each other from various sources to enhance their respective programs or operating systems. This implies an openness to share and to benefit from the wisdom gained by others. Yet it also presupposes that each programmer has learned basic skills of a specific programming language as a foundation on which to build and to include the insights of others. Just so, InterSpiritual Meditation builds on the wisdom and processes of many diverse contemplative traditions. As with computer programmers, InterSpiritual meditators will benefit from a grounding in a single contemplative tradition as a foundation for open-source spiritual inquiry, sharing, and adaptation.

INTERSPIRITUAL MEDITATION
A SEVEN-STEP PROCESS

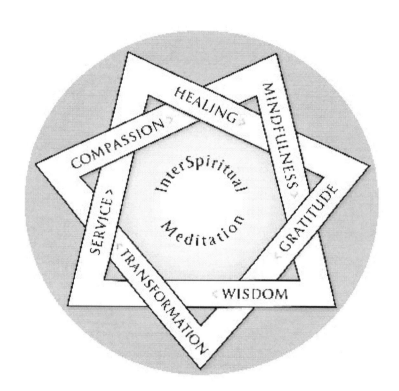

AN INTEGRATED PROCESS FOR
PERSONAL & GROUP PRACTICE

INTERSPIRITUAL MEDITATION – SEVEN-STEP CHART

	MENTAL STATE	PRAYER	ATTRIBUTES
1	Motivation	*"May I Be Healthy and Happy."*	Mind Body Spirit
2	Gratitude	*"May I Be Grateful for Life's Many Gifts."*	Remembrance Gratitude Trust Devotion Prayer Offering
3	Transformation	*"May I Be Transformed Into My Highest Ideal."*	Visualizing the Ideal Self-Assessment Confession Remorse Inward Love Forgiveness Surrender Commitment
4	Compassion (Intention)	*"May I Be Loving and Compassionate."*	Exchange Self for Others Reciprocity Universal Love

5	Mindfulness (Attention)	*"May I Be Focused and Mindful Through Breathing."*	Body Position Focus on Breath Concentration & Attention Recollection Patience Perseverance Observation ('Mental Spy') Quiescence
6	Meditation	*"May I Become Wise Through Meditation"*	Tranquil Focus Insight Non-Duality InterBeingness Equanimity Unity Absorption Transcendence Integration
7	Dedication	*"May I Serve All Beings with Compassion, Peace, and Wisdom"*	Visualize applying this in the coming day.

A BRIEF DESCRIPTION

THIS CONTEMPLATIVE PROCESS can be shared by people from many perspectives and traditions. It can be practiced alone and in community with others. It pulls together key elements of contemplation and meditation shared by many traditions. In this process we gather in the language of silence and experience inter-connectedness. Joining in stillness, we don't impose on others our own personal beliefs, rituals, or the names for our absolute truths, deities, or God. We honor and celebrate the wise and compassionate practices of all traditions. We discover a profound unity within our diversity. We flourish in the love, peace, compassion, gratitude, and strength of our shared wisdom. We are of one heart. Quietly, each in our own way, we join in the following seven stages together. The sound of a bell leads us from one stage to the next.

1. MOTIVATION: *May I Become Healthy and Happy*
   Physical, mental, and spiritual health are intertwined; meditation fosters their good health and happiness. We begin meditating with confidence and determination that it will help us heal the innermost causes of illness and suffering. We pray that InterSpiritual consciousness will help heal all beings.

2. GRATITUDE: *May I Be Grateful for Life's Many Gifts*
   With gratitude we invoke and honor our teachers, mentors, and great spiritual role models. We invite these great beings to remain present, and pray that they guide us. We express gratitude for life's challenges for it is through these that our wisdom and compassion grows. We remind ourselves about the blessings of friends, family, and the environment that nurtures and sustains us.

3. TRANSFORMATION: *May I Be Transformed Into My Highest Ideal*
   We imagine the highest purpose and potential for our lives. We acknowledge and confess our shortcomings, vowing to patiently persevere in our personal transformation. We vow to remove our inner obstacles and negativities. Without guilt, we forgive others and ourselves as we open to the transformative presence of love.

4. INTENTION: *May I Be Loving and Compassionate*

   We set our intention on love and compassion -- the transforming energy for the health and happiness of all. Knowing that happiness of ourselves and others are intertwined, we vow to help all beings to be free from the causes of their suffering.

5. MINDFULNESS: *May I Be Focused and Mindful Through Breathing*

   Mindfully, we concentrate on our breathing. This calms, clears, and focuses our mind. Thoughts, memories, and feelings are observed and released. We focus on our breath, drawing it into the heart-center of our being. Opening ourselves to the reciprocity of universal love, healing, and wisdom we establish the tranquil focus for deep meditation.

6. MEDITATION: *May I Become Wise Through Meditation*

   Meditation and contemplation are taught in many ways by many traditions. With sincere respect and appreciation for others and dedication to our own practice, we silently engage in our own meditation. Alone or in community, we deepen of our own wisdom as well as our InterSpiritual communion with other diverse experiences of that which we call "sacred."

7. DEDICATION: *May I Serve All Beings with Compassion, Peace, and Wisdom*

   Visualizing our family, friends, colleagues, antagonists, and all beings throughout the world we rededicate ourselves to becoming servants of peace, justice, and environmental health. May this meditation help us to engage together in the world with patient kindness and wise compassion.

STEP ONE

MOTIVATION

"May I Be Healthy and Happy"

STEP ONE: MOTIVATION – *"May I Be Healthy and Happy"*

IT IS NOT EASY to sustain a regular practice of meditation. Therefore we need a strong motivation. For some, this personal goal of health and happiness may seem selfish and not worthy of a compassionate contemplative practice. Whether we admit it or not however, our own health and happiness is an unavoidable goal. Achieving it, as we will see, entails a profound process of transformation that is entailed in the six steps that follow. So our prayer for health and happiness is a practical and honest place for most of us to begin. Looking after our own health and happiness can provide the motivational starting place we need to sustain a regular practice of contemplation and meditation.

Even the neurological and medical sciences are proving the value of a regular practice. Here are two quotes to illustrate this point:

> "Meditation has been shown to reduce both the experience of chronic pain and its inhibition of everyday activities. Pain-related drug utilization was decreased and activity levels and self-esteem increased."
> —Jon Kabat-Zinn

> "Not only do studies show that meditation is boosting their immune system, but brain scans suggest that it may be rewiring their brains to reduce stress… Ten million American adults now say they practice some form of meditation regularly."
> —J. Stein[2]

For additional information on Step One, please refer to the book *InterSpiritual Meditation*. The following verses, poems, and quotes are provided to stimulate your journaling.

---

2 Stein, J. (2003) "The Science of Meditation," *TIME Magazine*, August 4: 48-56.

Poems, Stanzas, and Scriptural Passages

Below are inspirational verses from various traditions to help stimulate your own contemplation and journaling for Step One.

"The Law of Reversed Effect"

We hate misery, but love its causes.
We love happiness, but refuse to cultivate its causes.
— Alan Watts

"Four Worldly Dharmas"

Gain and Loss: When we seek things to make us happy, we are often frustrated in the attempt, angry when they don't, or saddened by their loss; therefore, we suffer.

Pleasure and Pain: When we seek happiness through sensual pleasure, our longing and attachment to the pleasure, or sadness from the pain of unfulfilled expectations inevitably leads to pain and suffering.

Praise and Scorn: When we seek happiness through the praise of others, this praise eventually leads to scorn and jealousy, which are the result of the ignorance that gave rise to the desire for praise in the first place.

Fame and Ill Repute: When we seek happiness through fame, the examination of our most minute flaws becomes the occupation of others, and we become the target for their criticism.
— Edward W. Bastian

Judaism & Christianity

Happy is the one who finds wisdom
And gains understanding.
— *Proverbs* 3:13

HINDUISM

Instill in us a wholesome, happy mind
With goodwill and understanding.
Then shall we ever delight in your friendship
Like cows who gladly rejoice in meadows green.
This is my joyful message.
— *Rig Veda* X, 25:1

BUDDHISM

May I be well.
May I be happy.
May I enjoy good health.
May I be peaceful.
May all my good purposes by fulfilled.

May all sentient beings everywhere,
In all realms, in all world systems, be well.
May they be happy.
May they enjoy good health.
May they be peaceful.
May all their good purposes be fulfilled.

— *Visuddhimagga* 9: 9-39

TAOISM

Health is the greatest possession.
Contentment is the greatest treasure.
Confidence is the greatest friend.
Non-being is the greatest joy.
— Unknown

QUESTIONS TO STIMULATE CONTEMPLATION AND JOURNALING

The following questions are posed to stimulate your journaling. Please add you own questions or rephrase these so they have greater personal meaning. Your journal writings will help you formulate your own personal contemplative focus for this step.

What is your definition for health and happiness?

Can constant, sustainable health and happiness come solely through external causes?

What changes in your inner life are required to be healthy and happy?

What is the relationship between a healthy mind, body, and spirit? How are they mutually dependent?

Do health and happiness require you to be loving, compassionate? Why or why not?

Do health and happiness require you to change your attitude and values? What changes are necessary?

Do health and happiness require you to change your diet and exercise, life habits, career, and hygiene? What are these?

Do health and happiness require you to change the quality of my mind and consciousness? What changes are required?

Do you need deep and abiding purpose and meaning for your life in order to be healthy and happy?

What is the purpose of contemplation and meditation in accomplishing these objectives?

YOUR CONTEMPLATIVE PRACTIVE

Please remember that the purpose of the above quotes and questions are to stimulate your writing in your journals. In your writing, please explore your own deepest personal conclusions as well as your beliefs that have been molded by your tradition, teachers, mentors, or role models. You might also do additional research on the internet, in books, and conversations with other teachers and students. Then, reflecting on your journal writings, create a brief summary that will be the contemplative focus for this step.

As you begin this step, say to yourself with total conviction: *"May I Be Healthy and Happy."* This is not only a prayer, but also your self-directed challenge to discover and activate the true inner causes of health and happiness. With this determination, engage in meditation to cultivate these causes and to eliminate the obstacles to health and happiness.

In your contemplation, bring to mind the summary of your journal writings and vow to actualize these in your life. By beginning this contemplation with a prayer, we open ourselves to the transformative power and support of the vast and untapped potential of consciousness and (if appropriate) our "higher power."

STEP ONE: JOURNALING

STEP ONE: JOURNALING

STEP ONE: JOURNALING

STEP ONE: JOURNALING

STEP ONE: JOURNALING

STEP ONE: JOURNALING

STEP TWO

GRATITUDE

*"May I Be Grateful for
Life's Many Gifts"*

STEP TWO: GRATITUDE – *"May I Be Grateful for Life's Many Gifts"*

EACH DAY OF our lives we have a choice whether we approach life with pessimism and resentment or optimism and gratitude. The attitude of gratitude does not require us to be Pollyannaish or romantic, rather it enables us to welcome the opportunities and blessings that flow from every pleasant or unpleasant situation, person, and event of our life. In this step of the meditation, we give rise to sincere gratitude for both life's opportunities and challenges for they are intertwined one with the other.

For additional information on this step, please refer to the book *InterSpiritual Meditation.* The following materials are provided to stimulate your journaling.

POEMS, STANZAS, AND SCRIPTURAL PASSAGES

Below are inspirational verses from various traditions to help inspire your own contemplation and journaling for Step Two.

NATIVE AMERICAN

O Great Spirit, whose voice I hear in the wind and whose breath gives life to all the world, hear me. I come before you, one of your many children. I am weak and small. I need your strength and wisdom. Let me walk in beauty and make my eyes ever behold the red and purple sunset; my ears sharp so I may hear your voice. Make me wise, so I may learn the things you have taught my people; the lessons you have hidden under every rock and leaf. I seek strength not to be superior to others, but to come to you with clean hands and straight eyes, so whenever life fades, like the fading sunset, my spirit will come to you without shame.   — Chief Yellow Lark Blackfoot

LACANDON MAYA

Before Grandfather Sun comes up,
I arise to offer sacred smoke
And prayers to the Maker and Shaper.
I send my prayers on the wind, to the four directions.
I ask Creator to take pity on humanity
For we are seeking our correct path.

I enter the Silence.
I listen to the great guardians,
Trees, without whose breath we cannot live.
I offer prayers of gratitude to the plants and nature,
For it is through nature that we are guided to the Infinite.
Nature is the good spirit that guides us
And shows us how to live in harmony and balance.

—Tezkalci Matorral Cachora, Yoeme/Lacandon Maya

BUDDHISM

You, Universally Honored.
Are a great benefactor.
By doing this rare thing,
You have taught and benefited us
Out of your compassion toward us;
I will never be able to repay your favors,
Even if I try for millions of kalpas;
I will never be able to repay your favors,
Even if I bow respectfully to you,
Offering my hands or feet and everything else;
I will never be able to repay your favors,
Even if I carry you on my head or shoulders
And respect you from the bottom of my heart
For as many kalpas as there is sand in the River Ganges.
— *The Lotus Sutra 4*

JUDAISM

It is good to give thanks unto the Lord,
To sing praises unto Your Name, Most High,
To proclaim Your loving-kindness in the morning,
And Your faithfulness every night.
— *Psalms 92: 1-2*

A SIMPLE PRAYER

Thank you *God* for all that grows,
Thank you for the sky's rainbows,
Thank you for the stars that shine,
Thank you for these friends of mine,
Thank you for the moon and sun,
Thank you *God* for all you've done!
— Source Unknown

OUR FAMILY PRAYER (UNIVERSAL)

We give thanks for our variety of skills and interests;
For our different ways of thinking, moving and speaking;
For common hardships and common hopes;
For this family gathered here;
For living together and eating together;
For all our good times, and not so good times;
For growing up and growing older;
For wisdom deepened by experience;
For rest and leisure;
For the privilege of work;
For time made precious by its passing;
For all that has been,
And all that will be;
For all these blessings, we give thanks.
— Bastian/Winslow/Irons Family Prayer from unknown source

SECULAR

Gratitude unlocks the fullness of life. It turns what we have into enough, and more. It turns denial into acceptance, chaos to order, confusion to clarity. It can turn a meal into a feast, a house into a home, a stranger into a friend. Gratitude makes sense of our past, brings peace for today, and creates a vision for tomorrow. — Melody Beattie

We clasp the hands of those that go before us,
And the hands of those who come after us.
We enter the little circle of each other's arms
And the larger circle of lovers,
Whose hands are joined in a dance,
And the larger circle of all creatures,
Passing in and out of life,
Who move also in a dance,
To a music so subtle and vast that no ear hears it
Except in fragments
— Wendell Berry

Praying
It doesn't have to be
the blue iris, it could be
weeds in a vacant lot, or a few
small stones; just
pay attention, then patch
a few words together and don't try
to make them elaborate, this isn't
a contest but the doorway
into thanks, and a silence in which
another voice may speak.
— Mary Oliver

Questions to Stimulate Contemplation and Journaling

When we examine the teachings of the world's contemplative traditions we begin to see concurrence regarding specific mental attributes to be cultivated in the practice of gratitude. Here, I have listed seven of these as a foundation for your journaling and contemplation. These are remembrance, thankfulness, trust and faith, devotion, prayer, offering, and sacrifice.

For each of the mental attributes I have included a series of questions to stimulate your journaling. The following questions are posed to stimulate your journaling. Your journal writings will help you formulate your own personal contemplation focus for this step.

Remembrance

In this step of our meditation, we remember with profound gratitude some of the people and ideals that help us to develop sustainable health, happiness, purpose, and meaning.

Who and/or what are those people and principles that truly help you to develop deep and sustainable health and happiness?

What are the positive aspects in your life and your relationships for which you can be grateful?

What are the elements of nature, the earth, and the universe that give you life, and sustain and enliven you?

What are challenges in your life that can help you to deepen your wisdom, patience, compassion, and life perspective?

Who are the teachers, exemplars, and role models (either contemporary or historic) whose teachings have enriched your life and giving it meaning?

What are the teachings, the principles, the truths, the perspectives that give reason, meaning and purpose to your life?

Thankfulness

A completely sincere and explicit attitude of thanks refines our internal mental environment. It creates the mental foundation wherein the objects of our gratitude can be internalized, embodied, or integrated. Therefore, having first remembered those beings and things that help us to achieve sustainable health, happiness, wisdom, compassion, and spiritual direction, we now give sincere thanks to them from depths of our mind and heart.

TRUST

To endure and overcome the obstacles we need abiding faith that the goal will be worth the effort. Now, having remembered and given thanks to those that help us to live a happy and healthy life with meaning and purpose, we generate and renew our trust and faith that these will help fulfill our goals.

DEVOTION

In order to achieve our personal goals and ideals, we must be very devoted to them. Devotion is a profound and practical mental quality that fuels the commitment, perseverance, patience, and energy we need to actualize our highest ideals. At this stage, we bring forth a deep and sincere devotion to actualize and sustain those ideals and practices in which we have placed our trust and faith.

PRAYER

The word "prayer" connotes the most sincere and fervent wish that a human being can make. It signifies our humble openness to receive the blessings from that which we consider the source of divine wisdom, love and ultimate fulfillment. Whether prayer is directed to another being, to the depths of our own consciousness, to God, or to a universal power, we are evoking a deep personal wish that is far more profound than the mundane desires that generally occupy our minds. Prayer activates the potential of our essential being to actualize our most profound and benevolent aspirations for ourselves and others. The efficacy of prayer can be measured in our sense of peace, in our steadfast determination to achieve even the most difficult tasks, and our capacity to help comfort and heal others.

OFFERING

A material, mental, or virtual offering is a powerful way to seal and prove our commitment and devotion to our highest ideal. It is a powerful psychological intention to actualize the teachings of those to whom we are grateful.

What are you willing to offer in order to live your life in alignment with the teachings and ideals of those to whom you are grateful?

What are you willing to offer to achieve your highest life goals?

YOUR CONTEMPLATIVE PRACTICE

Please remember that the purpose of the above quotes, questions, and attributes of gratitude is to stimulate your contemplative writing in your journals. In your writing, please explore your own deepest personal insights as well as your beliefs that have been molded by your tradition, teachers, mentors, or role models. You might also do additional research on the internet, in books, and conversations with other teachers and students. Then, reflecting on your writings, create a brief summary that will be the contemplative focus for this step.

As you begin this step, say to yourself with total conviction: *"May I Be Grateful for Life's Many Gifts."* This is not only a prayer, but also your self-directed challenge to fully appreciate both the easy and difficult gifts of life for which we can be grateful. With this determination, engage in meditation to cultivate gratitude and to eliminate the negative states of mind that lead to pessimism, depression, antipathy, and self-doubt.

In your contemplation, bring to mind the summary of your journal writings and vow to actualize these in your life. Here, in answer to our prayer, we open ourselves to the transformative power and support of the vast and untapped potential of consciousness and (if appropriate) our "higher power."

STEP TWO: JOURNALING

Step Two: Journaling

STEP TWO: JOURNALING

STEP TWO: JOURNALING

STEP TWO: JOURNALING

STEP TWO: JOURNALING

STEP THREE

TRANSFORMATION

*"May I Be Transformed
Into My Highest Ideal"*

STEP THREE: TRANSFORMATION –

"May I Be Transformed Into My Highest Ideal"

IN ORDER TO MAKE positive changes in our lives, it is very helpful to visualize our ideal life goals, to assess our present condition, to confess our shortcomings, to feel remorse, to forgive and commit to a fresh start. Please contemplate the following questions and formulate your transformative commitments in your journal. Your contemplative writing will provide the foundation for your personal contemplation on transformation, the third step in our meditation.

For additional information on this step, please refer to the book *InterSpiritual Meditation*. The following materials are provided to stimulate your journaling.

POEMS, STANZAS, AND SCRIPTURAL PASSAGES

Below are inspirational verses from various traditions to help stimulate your own contemplation and journaling on transformation.

TAOIST PRECEPTS

~Becoming One with the Tao~

1. Practice inaction and effortless flow (wu wei);
2. Be supple and soft;
3. Guard the feminine, and don't be first;
4. Be nameless;
5. Practice purity and tranquility;
6. Engage in only good and skillful behavior;
7. Practice desirelessness;
8. Be contented;
9. Yield and withdraw.

HINDUISM

Just as a caterpillar,
Having reached the end of a blade of grass
And approaching another one, collects itself
[For making the transition],
Even so this atman, having discarded
The body and overcome ignorance,
Approaching another one
Collects itself [for making the transition].

This atman is in truth Brahman,
Consisting of consciousness,
Desire and desirelessness,
Righteousness and unrighteousness.
According to one's deeds,
According to one's behavior,
So one becomes.

Just as a goldsmith,
Taking an object of gold,
Fashions it afresh into another
New and more beautiful form,
So the atman, discarding this body
And dispersing its ignorance,
Makes for itself another
New and more beautiful form:
That of the Fathers, the spirits, the Gods,
Prajapati, Brahman, or of other beings.

The one who does good becomes good,
The one who does evil becomes evil.
One becomes virtuous by virtuous action
And evil by evil action.
But others say that
The human being consists of desire;
As is the desire, so is the intention,
And as is the intention, so is the action.
And whatever the action, that is what is obtained.

— *Brhadaranyaka Upanishad*, IV

CHRISTIANITY

Come to know the One
In the presence before you
And everything hidden from you will be revealed....
When you are able
to make two become one,
the inside like the outside,
and the outside like the inside
the higher like the lower,
so that a man is no longer male,
and a woman, female,
but male and female become a single whole...
Then you shall enter in.

— *Gospel of Thomas*, Logion 22

ISLAM - SUFIISM

Steadfast keep thy strength of heart,
For desires not to divert thy heart.
Concentrate thy powers and might,
For this is the meaning of life.
Purify thy heart in Truth,
Thy mirror is then cleansed and pure.
Thyself unite, for the call Divine,
To reveal in thee all life.

When the heart is pure and clear,
To heaven its journey's then.
When God unfolds thy heart,
Mirror of heart reflects thy lord.
Selfless and pure when life be thine,
Salek of religion as Mohammad doth Shine.
United with God thy life is blessed,
In solitude of heart thou findest faith.

— Hazrat Shah Maghsoud Sadegh Angha,
The Epic of Existence

BUDDHISM

It is just like what happens when all the kernels,
The husks of which have not yet been washed away,
Are disdained by someone who is impoverished,
And said to be something to be discarded.
But although the outside seems like something useless,
The inside is genuine and not to be destroyed.
After the husks are removed,
It becomes food fit for a king.
I see that all kinds of beings
Have a buddhagarbha *(Buddha Nature)* hidden by klesas.
I preach the removal of those things
To enable them to attain universal wisdom.
Just as I have a Tathagata nature,
So do all beings.
When they develop it and purify it,
They quickly attain the highest path.

— *The Tathagatagarbha Sutra*

QUESTIONS TO STIMULATE CONTEMPLATION AND JOURNALING

When we examine the teachings of the world's contemplative traditions we begin to see concurrence regarding specific mental attributes to be cultivated in the process of transformation. I have included over thirty of these in the seven steps of InterSpiritual Meditation.

Here in Step Three, I have included six of these mental attributes to help you accelerate the process of self-transformation. These are: imagining the ideal, self-assessment, confession, remorse, forgiveness, and commitment. Each of these is defined in "InterSpiritual Meditation." To help you contemplate these, I have included a series of questions pertaining to each.

The following questions are posed to stimulate your journaling about each of these mental attributes to be cultivated. Your journal writings will help you to explore and to cultivate these mental attributes as the foundation for your personal contemplative process.

IMAGINE THE IDEAL

Who is the person that you most admire and whose qualities you would like to emulate?

What are the qualities of being that you most want to manifest in your life?

What contribution to the world would you most like to make?

What is your deepest purpose for life?

What way of life and inner being would give your life ultimate meaning?

SELF-ASSESSMENT

From the depths of your heart, what do you most want to become or to manifest in your life?

Who or what are the role models for you to emulate?

What must you learn and who can teach you?

What internal changes are required to accomplish this?

What external life changes are required to accomplish this?

What qualities do you need to cultivate for this transformation?

What obstacles or negativities do you need to overcome or eliminate?

CONFESSION

What is your present condition with respect to your transformative goals?

What things are you doing, thinking, and saying that are not in line with your ideal?

What specific examples of these non-conforming thoughts, words, and actions can you bring to mind just now?

Why are these not consistent with your ideal way of being?

REMORSE

How do you feel regarding your thoughts, words, and actions that do not measure up to your higher standards?

Are you making excuses, or rejecting remorse for fear of poor self-image or esteem?

Are you confusing debilitating, unhealthy self-judgment with objective observation of your behaviors needed to reach your goals?

FORGIVENESS AND INWARD LOVE

Are you able to forgive yourself and not hang on to debilitating guilt?

Are you able to forgive others who might be related or complicit in your unsatisfactory thoughts, words, and actions?

Are you able to love and care for yourself just as you would another personal for whom you have unconditional love?

Are you able to forgive yourself without weakening your resolve for transformation?

COMMITMENT

Are you fully committed to transformation?

Are you willing to do what it takes to make the changes you desire?

What are the internal obstacles that weaken your resolve?

What are the temptations that lure you away from your goals?

Why do these temptations seem to be superior that your ideals?

Why are these higher ideals superior to your old mental, verbal, and behavior habits?

YOUR CONTEMPLATIVE PRACTICE

Please remember that the purpose of the above quotes and questions is to stimulate your writing in your journals. In your writing, please explore your own deepest personal insights as well as your beliefs that have been molded by your tradition, teachers, mentors, or role models. You might also do additional research on the internet, in books, and conversations with other teachers and students. Then, reflecting on your writings, create a brief summary that will be the contemplative focus for this step.

As you begin this step, say to yourself with total conviction: *"May I Be Transformed Into My Highest Ideal."* This is not only a prayer, but also your self-directed challenge to achieve your highest potential, to become your ideal being, and to actualize the qualities you most admire. With this determination, engage in meditation to become transformed and to eliminate the negative states of mind that prevent your transformation.

Depending on your way of looking at it, transformation might entail removing the coverings of your natural purity, eliminating obstacles preventing you from fulfilling your highest potential, or gradually accumulating qualities that you revere. However you look at transformation, the process inevitably entails a combination of emptying out and filling up. We empty out our false sense of self, our negative emotions, and our ignorance. We fill up with the positive and virtuous qualities such as: love, compassion, wisdom, unity, and that which we call the sacred or divine.

In your contemplation, bring to mind the summary of your journal writings on transformation, and vow to actualize these in your life. Here, in answer to your prayer, open yourself to the transformative power and support of the vast and untapped potential of consciousness and (if appropriate for you) a "higher power."

STEP THREE: JOURNALING

STEP THREE: JOURNALING

Step Three: Journaling

STEP THREE: JOURNALING

STEP THREE: JOURNALING

STEP THREE: JOURNALING

STEP FOUR

COMPASSION
(INTENTION)

*"May I Be Loving
and Compassionate"*

STEP FOUR: COMPASSION (INTENTION) – *"May I Be Loving and Compassionate"*

THE INTENTION OF love and compassion are at the heart of all great spiritual and contemplative traditions. They are the foundation for the health and happiness for ourselves and others. They are the divine intentions for truly spiritual contemplative practice. Since there are times when love and compassion don't spontaneously flow from our hearts, contemplative journaling and practice can help us engender them. The verses and questions that follow are meant to inspire and stimulate your journaling on love and compassion so that they might spontaneously arise in your daily practice.

For additional information on this step, please refer to the book *InterSpiritual Meditation.* The following materials are provided to stimulate your journaling.

POEMS, STANZAS, AND SCRIPTURAL PASSAGES

Below are inspirational verses from various traditions to help stimulate your own contemplation and journaling on love and compassion.

CHRISTIANITY

Love is patient, love is kind;
It does not envy, it does not boast,
It is not proud, nor is it rude;
It is not self-seeking, nor easily angered,
It keeps no record of wrongs.
Love does not delight in evil,
But rejoices in the truth.
Love bears all things, believes all things,
Hopes all things, and endures all things.
Love never ends.
— St. Paul in his *First Letter to the Corinthians*

And God said to the soul:
I desired you before the world began.
I desire you now
As you desire me.
And where the desires of two come together
There love is perfected

How the Soul Speaks to the Soul
Lord, you are my lover,
My longing,
My flowing stream,
My sun,
And I am your reflection.

How God Answers the Soul
It is my nature that makes me love you often,
For I am love itself.
It is my longing that makes me love you intensely,
For I yearn to be loved from the heart.
It is my eternity that makes me love you long,
For I have no end.

— Mechthild of Madgeburg, from *Teachings of the Christian Mystics*

BUDDHISM

May I be a guide for those who journey on the road.

May I be a boat, a raft, a bridge

For those who wish to cross the water.

May I be an isle for those who yearn for land,

A lamp for those who long for light;

For all who need a resting place, a bed;

For those who need a servant, may I be their slave.

May I be the wishing jewel, the vase of wealth,

A word of power and the supreme healing,

May I be the tree of miracles,

For every being the abundant cow.

Thus, for everything that lives,

As far as are the limits of the sky,

May I be constantly their source of livelihood

Until they pass beyond all sorrow.

— *Way of the Bodhisattva, 3:18-20, 22*

HINDUISM

Love is the firstborn,
Loftier than the Gods;
You, O Love, are the eldest of all,
Altogether mighty.
To you we pay homage!

Greater than the breadth
Of Earth and Heaven
Or of Waters and Fire,
You, O Love, are the eldest of all,
Altogether mighty.
To you we pay homage!

Greater than the quarters and directions,
The expanses and vistas of the sky,
You, O Love, are the eldest of all,
Altogether mighty.
To you we pay homage!

Greater than all things moving and inert,
Than the Ocean, O Passion,
You, O Love, are the eldest of all,
Altogether mighty.
To you we pay homage!

Beyond the reach of Wind or Fire,
The Sun or the Moon,
You, O Love, are the eldest of all,
Altogether mighty.
To you we pay homage!

In many a form of goodness, O Love,
You show your face.
Grant that these forms may penetrate
Within our hearts.
Send elsewhere all malice!

—*Atharva Veda IX*: 2:19-21, 23-25

JUDAISM

You shall not take vengeance or bear a grudge against your kinsfolk.
Love your neighbor as yourself...

—*Leviticus* 19:18

The stranger who resides with you shall be to you as one of your citizens;
you shall love him as yourself, for you were strangers in the land of Egypt.
—*Leviticus* 19:34

That which is hateful to you, do not do to your fellow.
That is the whole Torah; the rest is the explanation; go and learn.
—*Talmud*, Shabbat 31a

ISLAM — SUFISM

The sickness of love is not like any other;
Love is the astrolabe of God's mysteries.
Whether Love is from heaven or earth,
it points to God.
However I may try to explain it,
When faced with Love itself
I'm ashamed of my explanations.
Whatever the tongue can make clear,
Love's silence is better.

And though the pen wanted badly to write,
when it came to Love its nib split apart.
When it was the turn of the Intellect
To unfold the meaning of Love,
It stumbled like a donkey in the mud.
In the end only Love
Could explain itself
And what it is to be a lover.

—*Mathnawi I*, 110-111 of Jalaluddin Rumi[3]

My soul is a furnace
happy with the fire.
Love, too, is a furnace,
and ego its fuel

—*Mathnawi II*, 1376-7 of Jalaluddin Rumi[4]

---

3   translated by Camille and Kabir Helminski in *Rumi Daylight*
4   translated by Camille and Kabir Helminski in *Jewels of Rumi*

Questions to Stimulate Contemplation and Journaling

The world's contemplative traditions often concur about the types of mental attributes and methods to be cultivated for generating compassion. Below, I have listed some of these along with questions to stimulate your journaling and contemplative regarding each. These attributes and methods include: sympathy and empathy, equalizing self and others, realizing the interdependence between person happiness and the happiness of others, the natural law of reciprocity, and the universal pervasiveness of love and compassion.

Your journal writings will help love and compassion to emerge even when we don't feel that way. They will help provide a focus of love and compassion for Step Four of *InterSpiritual Meditation*. First, you might begin by exploring answers to these questions.

What is your definition for love and compassion?

Do these arise solely from inside your self or are they a universal quality that you tap into?

Describe how love and compassion arise in you: Are they dependent on a desirable object or person. Or do they arise when you see someone who is suffering, in danger, or deprived of their basic human rights?

Is your love and compassion conditional, or does it arise naturally and spontaneously without conditions?

How is your own health and happiness connected with the love and compassion others have for you?

How is the well-being and happiness of others intertwined with your own?

Do you gain greater happiness when you selfishly get what you want or when you help another person get what he or she needs?

Sympathy and Empathy

Are you able to sympathize with the suffering of others by relating it to your own experience?

Are you able to empathize heart to heart with others with a spontaneous wish to help relieve their suffering and bring them happiness?

Equalize Self & Others

When you lack spontaneous compassion for a difficult person, have you tried changing places with them?

When you see the world through the eyes of another, are you better able to see the causes of their suffering and feel love and compassion toward them?

Are you able to objectively look at your own suffering and feel the same sympathy, empathy, love and compassion that you would feel for another person who is suffering?

What does it feel like when you put yourself in another's shoes to feel their suffering, to realize why they might be suffering, and why they might be acting negatively towards you?

What does it feel like when you "trade places" with others who are suffering and see the world through their eyes?

How are you able to see yourself in others and others in you? What changes to you observe in yourself when you see that we all share the challenges inherent in the human condition?

When you do have empathy, how are your negative feelings affected toward those you have aversion towards? Does this empathy motivate you to find ways to alleviate the causes of their internal pain or negative behavior?

How does this empathy help you to practice the Golden Rule – "Do unto others as you would have them do unto you?"

INTERDEPENDENCE AND UNIVERSAL RECIPROCITY

How do you perceive the causal and interdependent nature of things?

How do you understand the interdependence between personal happiness and the happiness of others?

How does interdependence entail reciprocity, whereby all things are serving the needs of others?

What is your way of describing the natural state of universal reciprocity?

How do you describe the inter-permeability between living beings?

What words might you use to describe or express the possible interrelationship between universal reciprocity and universal love and compassion?

UNIVERSAL ESSENCE

How is it possible that love and compassion could be essential qualities of the universe?

How would you relate love and compassion with your sense of God, ground of being, or higher power.

Your Contemplative Practice

Please remember that the purpose of the above quotes and questions is to stimulate your writing in your journals. In your writing, please explore your own deepest personal insights as well as your beliefs that have been molded by your tradition, teachers, mentors, or role models. You might also do additional research on the internet, in books, and conversations with other teachers and students. Then, reflecting on your writings, create a brief summary that will serve as the contemplative focus for this step.

As you begin this step, say to yourself with total conviction: *"May I Be Loving and Compassionate."* This is not only a prayer, but also your self-directed challenge to actualize the qualities of love and compassion twenty-four hours a day, seven days a week for the rest of your life – indeed your eternal existence. With this determination, engage in meditation to become loving and compassionate and to eliminate the negative states of mind that prevent you from actualizing these.

In your contemplation, bring to mind the summary of your journal writings and vow to actualize these in your life. Here, in answer to our prayer, we open ourselves to the transformative power and support of the vast and untapped potential of consciousness and (if appropriate for you) our "higher power."

STEP FOUR: JOURNALING

STEP FOUR: JOURNALING

STEP FOUR: JOURNALING

STEP FOUR: JOURNALING

STEP FOUR: JOURNALING

STEP FOUR: JOURNALING

STEP FIVE

MINDFULNESS
(ATTENTION)

*"May I Be Focused and
Mindful Through Breathing"*

STEP FIVE: MINDFULNESS (ATTENTION) –
"May I Be Focused and Mindful Through Breathing"

IN MANY SPIRITUAL TRADITIONS, subtle breath is equated with spirit and the vital source of life. There are many types of meditations on breathing and these can be used for healing, stress reduction, physical strength, tranquility, equanimity, one-pointed concentration, transcendent states of consciousness, unity with the divine, and for emptying the obstacles to wisdom, compassion, and freedom. Breath meditations are often a prelude to deep states of meditative absorption and realization.

Breathing connects us to the interdependent reciprocal nature of all existence. For example, we breathe in the oxygen produced by plants and we exhale the carbon dioxide that plants need to survive. The microscopic living cells that compose our body are nourished by the oxygen we breathe in. And their health is tantamount to the health of our body. In this way, breathing connects our inner and outer worlds.

The mental skill called "Mindfulness" is often associated with Buddhism, but it also can be found either implicit or explicit in many other contemplative traditions. The term can include various attributes including the attention, recollection, concentration, and observation, each of which carry slight different connotations. The following quotes and questions are meant to stimulate your contemplation on these attributes of mindfulness and to help you create a focus on breath and breathing in a way that has personal meaning and benefit.

POEMS, STANZAS, AND SCRIPTURAL PASSAGES

Below are inspirational verses from various traditions to help stimulate your own contemplation and journaling for Step Five.

JUDAISM

The heavens are shaped by Yah's Word,
Yah's breath gives life to all its being.
— *Psalms* 33:6

The Sovereign Lord says to these bones:
I will make breath enter you,
And you will come to life.
— *Ezekiel* 37:5

And Y-H-V-H, God, formed the human, of the dust from the soil,
he blew into his nostrils the breath of life and
the human became a human being.
— *Genesis* 2:7

BUDDHISM

A bhikkhu having gone to the forest,
To the foot of a tree, or a solitary place,
Sits down cross-legged, the body erect,
And directs the mind to the object of mindfulness;
Then, with mindfulness, breathes in and breathes out:
Inhaling a long breath — "I inhale a long breath,"
Exhaling a long breath — "I exhale a long breath,"
Inhaling a short breath — "I inhale a short breath,"
Exhaling a short breath — "I exhale a short breath";
"Aware of this whole body of breath, I breathe in,"
"Aware of this whole body of breath, I breathe out,"
"Calming the process of breathing, I breathe in,"
"Calming the process of breathing, I breathe out,"
Thus does the bhikkhu train awareness.
— *Mahasatipatanasutta*

HINDUISM

Praise to your coming and your going, Breath,
Praise to your rising and your settling, Breath!

Praise to you, Breath of Life,
For both breathing in and out!
For turning to this side and to that,
Praise to all of you, everywhere!

Breath of Life, grant your blessed form
To us that we may live!
Give us your healing power!

The Breath of Life cares for all beings
Like a parent their child;
Master of all life, breathing or not.

We breathe in, we breathe out,
Even within the womb.
Quickened and enlivened by you,
And you bring us to birth!

Breath of Life, please do not forsake me.
You are, indeed, everything that I am.
As the embryo of all potential,
I bind myself to you that I may live!

— *Atharva Veda XI*, 4:1-10, 14, 26

CHRISTIANITY

Truly, truly, I say unto you,
Except a person be born
Of water and of the spirit-breath,
They cannot enter into the kingdom of God.
— *John* 3:5

ISLAM

Wherever I shine the lamplight of Divine breath,
there the difficulties of a whole world are resolve
The darkness which the earthly sun did not remove,
becomes through My breath a bright morning.

—*Mathnawi I*, 1941-2 of Jalaluddin Rumi[5]

TAOISM

Empty yourself of everything.
Let the mind become still.
The ten thousand things rise and fall
While the Self watches their return.
They grow and flourish
And then return to the source.
Returning to the source is stillness,
Which is the way of nature.
— Lao Tzu, *Tao Te Ching*

---

5   translated by Camille and Kabir Helminski in *Rumi Daylight*

QUESTIONS TO STIMULATE CONTEMPLATION AND JOURNALING

The teachings of the world's contemplative traditions often concur regarding the seminal importance of breath and breathing. Below, I have listed six of the mental attributes to be cultivated around the practice of breathing and focus on breath. These include: body position, attention, concentrated focus, patience, inner observation or vigilance, and recollection.

  The questions relating to each of these six mental attributes are meant to help you cultivate mindfulness through breathing. Please journal your thoughts and insights as a foundation for your own meditation.

BODY POSITION

Contemplation and meditation can take place in a variety of body positions including sitting cross-legged on a cushion, sitting on a chair, walking, running, swimming, bicycling, or laying down.

Why is the right body position important for meditation?

What is your best body position (or positions) to help you to stay alert, focused, and relaxed?

Why is this position better than the others?

ATTENTION

Full attention to the object or purpose of meditation is important in many traditions and types of meditation.

Generally, do you find it challenging to focus your attention on one thing or task?

Is it easier for you to focus your attention on breath, a syllable, an image, a prayer, a physical movement, and sacred symbol, or a universal truth?

What resistance or challenges do you experience when you try to focus your attention?

What are the sacred and secular benefits of cultivating focused attention?

Are you willing to devote the your time and effort to cultivating attention?

How often are you willing to work at developing the attribute of focused attention?

CONCENTRATED FOCUS ON BREATH AND BREATHING

Concentration on breath and breathing is of seminal importance in many types of meditation as well as spiritual practice.

What does breath mean to you? Is it simply the air that you breathe in and out? Does breath have a sacred significance?

In relation to your personal spiritual or scientific orientation, how do understand breath beyond its simple physical necessity for daily life?

What types of physical and mental feelings or sensations emerge for you when you focus on your breathing?

What are the beneficial effects of focused breathing on your mind and body?

How does focus on breathing in and out help you to become calm and present in the moment?

How does focus on breath help you to deepen and expand your life experience both in meditation, in relationships, in work, in sports, etc?

PATIENCE

In mindfulness practice, patience does not refer to forbearance towards other people but to the inner workings of our own mind. If we try too hard with the unrealistic expectation of quick results, the benefits of meditation will elude us. Without patience, meditation itself can be a stressful activity.

How do you define the meaning of patience?

Do you find yourself becoming impatient when it is hard to focus on your breathing?

Do you become impatient when the tranquility of meditation alludes you?

What is the effect of impatience in your meditation?

What method do you use in your meditation to cultivate patience?

How would you describe the result of approaching meditation with patience rather than worrying that you won't immediately gain the results you expect?

INNER OBSERVATION OR VIGILANCE

Non-judgmental observation and vigilance of the internal mental and physical feelings, perceptions, sensations, emotions, memories, and desires is the ally of focused concentration. Without inner vigilance, our minds will wander aimlessly and our physical sensations will distract us. Distractions will prevent us from achieving calm meditational focus.

Why should you cultivate the capacity to observe the inner workings of your mind and body?

What are the benefits of inner observation and vigilance?

Are you committed to developing the capacity for inner observation and vigilance?

How do you understand the capacity of your mind for the parallel processing of thoughts, emotions, memory, and/or projection, along with simultaneous observation of these mental events?

What is your experience in your attempts to cultivate inner observation and vigilance?

Describe the quality of your observation and vigilance, your ability to notice the emergence of mental events, and your ability to return to the object of meditation?

OBSERVATION AND RECOLLECTION

Mental and physical distractions often impede our continued focus on the object or purpose of meditation. Therefore, in order to refocus our minds after inevitable distractions, we cultivate our capacity to mindfully observe recollect, remember, and return to the object or purpose of our meditation.

How is your recollection impeded by the incessant arising of thoughts, emotions, sensations, and memories?

What is the value in being able to mindfully observe distractions, and then to recollect or remember the object of meditation?

How would you describe your internal experience when you try to remember the object of meditation, for example: your breath, a syllable, a prayer, or an image?

How is your recollection impeded by the incessant arising of thoughts, emotions, sensations, and memories?

How can the cultivation of all these attributes of mindfulness improve your meditation?

How does mindful breathing help you to achieve mental calm and focus in daily life?

QUIESCENCE

Nearly all contemplative traditions emphasize (implicitly or explicitly) the importance of Mindful breathing because is enables the mind to become calm and focused. It is often described as a state of "quiescence" wherein the mind rests in blissful awareness and equanimity.

How do you see the value and purpose for a mental state of quiescence?

Do you think it is possible?

Have you had glimpses of this state in your own meditations or other life experiences?

What is the value of this state of being for your own happiness and health as well as your capacity to help others?

Are you willing to develop the capacity and discipline of mindful breathing to achieve this state of being?

Will you make this a regular daily practice?

YOUR CONTEMPLATIVE PRACTICE

Please remember that the purpose of the above quotes and questions is to stimulate your writing in your journals. In your writing, please explore your own deepest personal insights as well as your beliefs that have been molded by your tradition, teachers, mentors, or role models. You might also do additional research on the internet, in books, and conversations with other teachers and students. Then, reflecting on your writings, create a brief summary that will be your contemplative focus for this step.

What type of breathing practice will you develop? How will you cultivate the attributes listed above?

As you begin this step, say to yourself with total conviction: *"May I Be Focused and Mindful Through Breathing."* This is not only a prayer, but also your self-directed challenge to actualize mindfulness whether awake or sleeping. With this determination, engage in meditation to become mindful and to eliminate the negative states of mind that prevent you from actualizing the attributes of mindfulness.

In your contemplation, bring to mind the summary of your journal writings and vow to actualize these in your life. Here, in answer to our prayer, we open ourselves to the transformative power and support of the vast and untapped potential of consciousness and (if appropriate) our "higher power."

*S*TEP *F*IVE: *J*OURNALING

STEP FIVE: JOURNALING

STEP FIVE: JOURNALING

STEP FIVE: JOURNALING

STEP FIVE: JOURNALING

STEP FIVE: JOURNALING

STEP SIX

MEDITATION

*"May I Become Wise
Through Meditation"*

Step Six: Meditation –
"May I Become Wise Through Meditation"

By way of review and context, please recall that each of the first four steps in this seven step process are "contemplative." That is, they require deep and calm conceptual consideration regarding our motivation, transformation, gratitude, and compassionate intention. However, Step Five is called "meditative" because it entails and non-conceptual focus on our breath along with the capacity to observe distractions, remember the meditative object, i.e., our breath, and sustain our tranquil concentration. It is called "meditative" because there is no conceptualization taking place. Each of these steps gradually help to prepare our minds for Step Six.

In many traditions, the primary purpose of meditation is to cultivate non-conceptual wisdom. It is often regarded as a direct insight into the truth of existence and/or (depending on your religion or belief system) a state of unity with God or a sacred state of being. Wisdom cultivated through meditation is the foundation for personal liberation as well as wise, loving, and compassionate service in the world. Although each spiritual tradition may have its own name for the ultimate reality, its own specified goals, nevertheless there are similarities in the meditative processes leading to that goal. Because InterSpiritual Meditation is non-sectarian and inclusive, it does not specify a metaphysical goal. Rather it provides a universal process to help each person develop and actualize their own spiritual goal or purpose. In so doing, we celebrate the diversity of the profound contemplative states of consciousness found throughout the world.

The following poems, stanzas, and scriptural passages are provide to help you journal the purpose and focus of your meditation. Your meditation might be a continuation of mindful breathing in Step Five, it might come from a single tradition, or from a variety of traditions you have studied and practiced. This is your opportunity to articulate, summarize, and practice the meditation of your choosing. If you have collected inspirational writings from other sources, please add these to you journal.

For additional information on this step, please refer to the book *InterSpiritual Meditation.* The following materials are provided to stimulate your journaling.

POEMS, STANZAS, AND SCRIPTURAL PASSAGES

Below are inspirational verses from various traditions to help stimulate your own contemplation and journaling for Step Six.

CHRISTIANITY

If you want to pray,
Enter your inner room,
Close the door,
And pray to your Father in secret,
And your Father who sees in secret
Will reward you.

—*Mathew* 6:6[6]

Ah blessed absence of God,
How lovingly I am bound to you!
You strengthen my will in its pain
And make dear to me
The long hard wait in my poor body.
The nearer I come to you,
The more wonderfully and abundantly
God comes upon me.
In pride, alas, I can easily lose you,
But in the depths of pure humility, O Lord,
I cannot fall away from you.
For the deeper I fall, the sweeter you taste.

— Mechthild of Magdeburg[7]

---

6   This is the scriptural source for Centering Prayer (or Contemplative Prayer), taught by Father Thomas Keating

7   translated by Oliver Davies

"For He can well be loved, but he cannot be thought. By love he can be grasped and held, but by thought, neither grasped nor held. And therefore, though it may be good at times to think specifically of the kindness and excellence of God, and though this may be a light and a part of contemplation, all the same, in the work of contemplation itself, it must be cast down and covered with a cloud of forgetting. And you must step above it stoutly but deftly, with a devout and delightful stirring of love, and struggle to pierce that darkness above you; and beat on that thick cloud of unknowing with a sharp dart of longing love, and do not give up, whatever happens."

— *The Cloud of Unknowing*

Let nothing disturb you;
Let nothing make you afraid;
All things pass;
But God is unchanging'
Patience
is enough for everything.
You who have God
lack nothing.
God alone is sufficient.
— Teresa of Avila

TAOISM

Before heaven and earth
There was something nebulous
silent isolated
unchanging and alone
eternal
the Mother of All Things
I do not know its name
I call it Tao.
— Lao Tzu, *Tao Te Ching*

BUDDHISM

Just as a bird with undeveloped
Wings cannot fly in the sky,
Those without the power of higher perception
Cannot work for the good of living beings.
The merit gained in a single day
By one who possess higher perception
Cannot be gained even in a hundred lifetimes

By one without such higher perception.
Those who want swiftly to complete
The collections for full enlightenment
Will accomplish higher perception
Through effort, not through laziness.

Without the attainment of calm abiding,
Higher perception will not occur.
Therefore make a repeated effort
To accomplish calm abiding.

When the practitioner has gained calm abiding,
Higher perception will also be gained,
But without practice of the perfection of wisdom,
The obstructions will not come to an end.

— Atisha, *Lamp for the Path to Enlightenment*

HINDUISM

"One who meditates
On contemplation as Brahman,
Their freedom will extend to
The limits of the realm of contemplation....."
"But, sir, is there anything greater than contemplation?"
"Yes, there is something greater than contemplation."
"Then please, sir, tell me about it!"

"Wisdom, verily, is greater than contemplation.
For by wisdom one knows heaven and earth.
Air and atmosphere, water and fire,
Gods, human beings, and animals, grass and trees,
Right and wrong, true and false, pleasant and unpleasant,
Food and drink, this world and the other . . .
All these are known by wisdom.
Meditate on wisdom.

"One who meditates on wisdom as Brahman,
Attains the worlds of wisdom and of knowledge.
Their freedom will extend to the limits of the realm of wisdom,
One who meditates on wisdom as Brahman."

— *Chandogya Upanishad VII,* 6:1-7:2

SECULAR

Those who dwell among the beauties and mysteries of the earth are never alone
or weary of life…Those who contemplate the beauty of the earth find reserves of
strength that will endure as long as life lasts.
— Rachel Carson, *The Sense of Wonder*

ISLAM — SUFISM

Listen, O drop, give yourself up without regret,
and in exchange gain the Ocean.
Listen, O drop, bestow upon yourself this honor,
and in the arms of the Sea be secure.
Who indeed should be so fortunate?
An Ocean wooing a drop!
In God's name, in God's name, sell and buy at once!
Give a drop, and take this Sea full of pearls.

— *Mathnawi IV*, 2619-2622 of Jalaluddin Rumi[8]

What does it mean to learn the knowledge of God's Unity?

To consume yourself in the presence of the One.

If you wish to shine like day,

burn up the night of self-existence.

Dissolve in the Being who is everything.

You grabbed hold of "I" and "we,"

and this dualism is your ruin.

— *Mathnawi I*, 3009-12 of Jalaluddin Rumi[9]

8   translated by Camille and Kabir Helminski, *Jewels of Remembrance*
9   translated by Camille and Kabir Helminski in *Rumi Daylight*

Let your heart be in such a state that the existence or non-existence of anything is the same—that is, let there be no dichotomy of positive and negative. Then sit alone in a quiet place, free of any task or preoccupation, be it the reciting of the Qur'an, thinking about its meaning, concern over the dictates of religion, or what you have read in books—let nothing besides God enter the mind. Once you are seated in this manner, start to pronounce with your tongue, "Allah, Allah" keeping your thought on it.

Practice this continuously and without interruption; you will reach a point when the motion of the tongue will cease, and it will appear as if the word just flows from it spontaneously. You go on in this way until every trace of the tongue movement disappears while the heart registers the thought or the idea of the word.

As you continue with this invocation, there will come a time when the word will leave the heart completely. Only the palpable essence or reality of the name will remain, binding itself ineluctably to the heart.

Up to this point everything will have been dependent on your own conscious will; the divine bliss and enlightenment that may follow have nothing to do with your conscious will or choice. What you have done so far is to open the window, as it were. You have laid yourself exposed to what God may breathe upon you, as He has done upon his prophets and saints.

If you follow what is said above, you can be sure that the light of Truth will dawn upon your heart. At first intermittently, like flashes of lightning, it will come and go. Sometimes when it comes back it may stay longer than other times. Sometimes it may stay only briefly.

— Al-Ghazali

QUESTIONS TO STIMULATE YOUR CONTEMPLATION AND JOURNALING ON MEDITATION

Mature meditators often report that it has taken them may years before they experience regularly the fruit of their practice. The process of meditation, they say, is not always like a "Spiritual Jacuzzi!" Not only do we need to know the techniques and formulas for our chosen meditation, but we need strong and abiding rationale, faith, perseverance, and devotion for sustaining our practice.

It is also very helpful to ground ourselves in a specific practice and to work with a qualified teacher to gain a proper understanding and method before trying to mix and match a variety of practices. Once we are grounded in a specific practice, we might begin to integrate the wisdom of other traditions and practices into our own InterSpiritual practice.

Whether our meditation is proscribed by a teacher, a tradition, or of your own design, it is important for you to own it and take personal responsibility for it. It is unrealistic to expect that the meditation will be done to you, for you, and that sublime experiences will happen automatically without your full commitment and engagement. Meditation is an inner career that can accompany us throughout out lives. Our mind is like a garden and meditation is the process we use to tend, nurture, and make it healthy.

The world's contemplative traditions often concur about the general processes of meditation and the mental attributes to be cultivated in order to develop a mature practice. The following questions are posed to stimulate your contemplative journaling. Your journal writings will help you formulate your own personal focus for this step. In developing or refining your meditation, these questions might help you gain clarity, confidence, and consistency.

How would you describe the purpose of your meditation? For example, do you meditate to actualize your own innate potential and/or to acquire the attributes of a higher power?

What are the fundamental beliefs you bring into this meditation regarding, for example: the nature of your being, a higher power, the existence of God, or the nature of the universe?

How do you define or describe your sense of the absolute truth, for example: God, Allah, Brahman, the Tao, Universal Consciousness, Primordial Energy?

How do you define or describe the nature of your essential being, self, soul, or spirit?

What spiritual benefits do you hope for from meditation?

What is the state-of-being you hope will arise from meditation?

What psychological, emotional, or physical benefits do you hope will come from meditation?

What changes in your relationships and career do you hope will come from meditating?

Do you have full confidence that your meditation can help achieve the results you hope for?

Do you have full confidence in the teacher or tradition that is the source of your meditation?

How would you describe your own personal responsibility in the development and practice of your meditation?

CHOOSING THE RIGHT MEDITATION FOR YOU

As you attempt to refine your present meditation or find a meditation that is best for you, the following types of meditation might help you gain clarity. These questions are not meant to lead you to any particular answer or to imply that there is a right answer for all people.

TRANQUIL FOCUS

Tranquil focus is a necessary condition for meditation.

What type of meditation will help you gain tranquil focus? Will it involve movement (like Yoga, Tai Chi, Chi Gong, walking, dancing, running, etc? Will it require silence? Will it be better with a group or alone?

What is the best point of focus of your meditation? For example, is it your breath, unity, inter-being-ness, emptiness, God, Allah, Brahman, the Tao, nature, love, remembrance, prayer?

INSIGHT

Non-conceptual direct insight and sense of unity is the hallmark of many meditations.

How would you describe the sacred truth or divine state of being that your meditation will help you to realize directly?

EQUANIMITY

Are you hoping for a state of deep calm and equanimity from your meditation?

How do you relate the terms happiness, equanimity, and calm? Are they interchangeable, mutually inclusive, or independent of each other?

Do you fear equanimity because it might extinguish the vibrant highs and lows of life? Please explore this.

UNITY

What do the terms unity and oneness mean to you?

How do you relate to the terms unity and oneness? Are they states of mind or being that you would like to experience or achieve in meditation?

If these terms are not meaningful to you, how would you describe the state of consciousness, insight and realization you would like to actualize in meditation?

YOUR CONTEMPLATIVE PRACTICE

Please remember that the purpose of the above quotes and questions is to stimulate your writing in your journals. In your writing, please explore your own deepest personal insights as well as your beliefs that have been molded by your tradition, teachers, mentors, or role models. You might also do additional research on the internet, in books, and conversations with other teachers and students. Then, reflecting on your writings, create a brief summary that will be the contemplative focus for this step.

As you begin this step, say to yourself with total conviction: *"May I Become Wise Through Meditation."* This is not only a prayer, but also your self-directed challenge to enter into meditation in order to gain the insight and wisdom to serve the highest purposes of all beings. With this determination, we engage in our meditation to realize its highest benefits.

Before entering into your meditation bring to mind the summary of your journal writings and vow to actualize them. Here, in answer to our prayer, we open ourselves to the transformative power and support of the vast and untapped potential of consciousness and your personal sense of the divine of "higher power."

STEP SIX: JOURNALING

Step Six: Journaling

STEP SIX: JOURNALING

STEP SIX: JOURNALING

STEP SIX: JOURNALING

STEP SIX: JOURNALING

Step Seven

Dedication

"May I Serve All Beings with Compassion, Peace, and Wisdom"

STEP SEVEN: DEDICATION –

"May I Serve All Beings with Compassion, Peace, and Wisdom"

AS WE GRADUALLY begin to emerge from our meditation we rededicate ourselves to wise, loving, compassionate service to others. We do this with the implicit understanding that our own wellbeing is inextricably intertwined with our vow to help others. We visualize the coming days and the inevitable challenges we have with certain situations and people. Visualizing these, we "preload" the compassionate wisdom of our meditation into those future moments so we are prepared to meet them with the grace of our inner purpose. By doing this, we transform our approach to the everyday stresses of life. In order for our meditation to stay with us and be of lasting benefit, it is very important that we end our session with our commitment to infuse each moment of the coming days with gratitude, compassion, mindful breathing, and wisdom gained through meditation.

For additional information on this step, please refer to the book *InterSpiritual Meditation*. The following materials are provided to stimulate your journaling.

POEMS, STANZAS, AND SCRIPTURAL PASSAGES

Below are inspirational verses from various traditions to help stimulate your own contemplation and journaling for Step Seven.

BUDDHISM

And now as long as space endures,
As long as there are beings to be found,
May I continue likewise to remain
To drive away the sorrows of the world.

— *Way of the Bodhisattva*, 10:55

CHRISTIANITY

Lord, make me an instrument of your peace,
Where there is hatred, let me sow love;
where there is injury, pardon;
where there is doubt, faith;
where there is despair, hope;
where there is darkness, light;
where there is sadness, joy;

Divine Master, grant that I
may not so much seek to be consoled as to console;
to be understood as to understand;
to be loved as to love.

For it is in giving that we receive;
it is in pardoning that we are pardoned;
and it is in dying that we are born to eternal life.
— St. Francis of Assisi

NATIVE AMERICAN

We have come on a good road
Of loving one another
And sticking by one another.
At this time we will disperse,
So keep the good work
And love one another.
That is the road that we came from,
The road of life,
Nothing but good,
And have strong will power
To do all this.
And all this, it will be so.

— Slow Buffalo, Lakota Chief

O Great Spirit, whose voice I hear in the wind and whose breath gives life to all the world, hear me. I come before you, one of your many children. I am weak and small. I need your strength and wisdom. Let me walk in beauty and make my eyes ever behold the red and purple sunset; my ears sharp so I may hear your voice. Make me wise, so I may learn the things you have taught my people; the lessons you have hidden under every rock and leaf. I seek strength not to be superior to others, but to come to you with clean hands and straight eyes, so whenever life fades, like the fading sunset, my spirit will come to you without shame.   — Chief Yellow Lark Blackfoot

ISLAM

Abandon this sly plotting for a while:
live free a few moments before you die.

— *Mathnawi VI*, 4444 of Jalaluddin Rumi[10]

The Messenger of good tidings said, speaking symbolically,
"Die before you die, generous ones,
even as I have died before death
and brought this reminder from Beyond."
Become the resurrection of the spirit,
so you may experience the resurrection:
this becoming is necessary for seeing and knowing
the real nature of anything.
Until you become it, you will not know it completely,
whether it be light or darkness.
If you become Reason, you will know Reason perfectly;
if you become Love, you will know Love's flaming wick.

— *Mathnawi VI*, 754-758 of Jalaluddin Rumi[11]

---

10   translated by Camille and Kabir Helminski in *Jewels of Remembrance*
11   translated by Camille and Kabir Helminski in *Jewels of Remembrance*

JUDAISM

There is holiness when we strive to be true to the best we know.
There is holiness when we are kind to someone who cannot
possibly be of service to us.
There is holiness when we promote family harmony.
There is holiness when we forget what divides us and remember
what unites us.
There is holiness when we love truly and honestly and unselfishly.
There is holiness when we remember the lonely and bring cheer
into a dark corner. — Kedushah prayer

QUESTIONS TO STIMULATE CONTEMPLATION AND JOURNALING ON YOUR DEDICATION

The world's contemplative traditions concur on the importance of dedication. Here are a series of questions to stimulate your journaling on your personal dedication.

What qualities and attributes of this entire meditation will you bring into the coming day(s)? How will you carry these with you in each moment?

What are the relationships and who are the people in your life with whom your experience stress, unhappiness, unease, and anger? How will you bring the qualities and attributes of this meditation into your relationship with them?

What are the situations in which you become stressed, impatient, unhappy, and angry? How will you bring the attributes of this meditation into those situations?

What are the reoccurring worries in your life, whether they are people, finances, job, relationships, or uncertainty over the future?   How will you apply this meditation as an antidote to these?

How will you be mindful of, and monitor your own negative inner states mind that arise in these circumstances?

Your Contemplative Practice

Please remember that the purpose of the above quotes and questions is to stimulate your writing in your journals. In your writing, please explore your own deepest personal conclusions as well as your beliefs that have been molded by your tradition, teachers, mentors, or role models. You might also do additional research on the internet, in books, and conversations with other teachers and students. Then, reflecting on your writings, create a brief summary that will be the contemplative focus for this step.

As you begin this step, say to yourself with total conviction: *"May I Serve All Beings with Compassion, Peace, and Wisdom."* This is not only a prayer, but also your commitment to apply the personal benefits of meditation to the sustainable happiness of all beings, and to utilize the wisdom gained in meditation to alleviate their suffering.

As you enter into this final step in our meditation, bring to mind the summary of your journal writings and vow to actualize them.

STEP SEVEN: JOURNALING

STEP SEVEN: JOURNALING

STEP SEVEN: JOURNALING

STEP SEVEN: JOURNALING

STEP SEVEN: JOURNALING

STEP SEVEN: JOURNALING

GUIDELINES FOR GROUP INTERSPIRITUAL
DISCUSSION AND PRACTICE

GUIDELINES FOR INTERSPIRITUAL GROUP DISCUSSION

THE PRIMARY LANGUAGE of InterSpiritual dialog is silence. It is the soothing elixir that places each person and each tradition on neutral, reciprocal ground. In silence we are liberated from our fixed religious or non-religious identities and the words that distinguish one truth from another. We celebrate and welcome the diversity of our respective spiritual styles, traditions, and racial, gender, and ethnic diversities. Separately and jointly, we experience a wordless quality or essence of being that unites us.

> When I am liberated by silence, when I am no longer involved in
> the measurement of life, but in the living of it, I can discover a
> form of prayer in which there is effectively no distraction.
> — Thomas Merton

When we enter into conversation with each other it is important that we maintain this same gentle and kind quality of being. Openness implies vulnerability, therefore we must take great care with our intentions and our words. Opening up to and with each other is rare and delicate occurrence. Therefore we take great care not to cause another person's shy inner self to recede back into the shadows of his or her consciousness. We create a safe and supportive container within which this contemplative process can unfold.

The following are two sets of guidelines to help us help each other. The first is a list that applies specifically to InterSpiritual dialogues. It is based on ten years of work with contemplative teachers from many traditions with the Spiritual Paths Foundation. The second comes from the work of Parker Palmer that he calls Circles of Trust. Here he provides Touch Stones to guide our conversations and our 'way of being' with each other.

Guidelines Developed in Our Spiritual Paths Programs

- Embrace silence as a common language and the elixir of shared experience and expand your exclusive identity to one that is inclusive and universal.

- Genuinely celebrate and honor the diversity of all spiritual traditions.

- Soften the personal boundaries of fixed identity of your own religion and belief system and open your heart for sincere sharing and learning from the experiences of others.

- Do not respond to a statement by another person with disagreement, agreement, or affirmation. Simply listen compassionately, allowing the statement of another to rest in contemplative reflection and silence.

- Refrain from imposing or projecting your views on others' traditions, beliefs, or practices.

- Refrain from imposing a single universal truth on all religions and spiritual traditions that might not be shared by the traditions themselves.

- If you belong to a specific tradition, speak "from" it rather than "for" it.

- Be careful not to misappropriate, or lift out of context, a specific practice from one tradition and graft it onto another tradition or your practice, without knowing its indigenous meaning.

- Engage in contemplative, compassionate listening to draw out wisdom within each participant. Meditatively observe and release your inner judgments and impulse to react to their words.

Parker Palmer's Circles of Trust Touchstones

The following "Touchstones" were adapted from Parker Palmer's Touchstones for *Circles of Trust*. More information can be found in his book "A Hidden Wholeness," or at The Center for Courage and Renewal: www.couragerenewal.org.   Palmer's methodology provides an extremely important grounding for InterSpiritual dialog.

- *Extend and receive welcome.* People learn best in hospitable spaces. In this circle, we support each other's learning by giving and receiving hospitality**.**

- *Be present as fully as possible.* Be here with your doubts, fears, and failings, as well as your convictions, joys, and successes; your listening as well as your speaking.

- *What is offered in the circle is by invitation, not demand.* This is not a "share or die" event! During this time, do whatever your soul calls for, and know that you do it with our support. Your soul knows your needs better than we do.

- *Speak your truth in ways that respect other people's truth.* Our views of reality may differ, but speaking one's truth in a circle of trust does not mean interpreting, correcting, or debating what others say. Speak from your center to the center of the circle, using "I" statements, trusting people to do their own sifting and winnowing.

- *No fixing, no saving, no advising, and no setting each other straight.* This is one of the hardest guidelines for those of us in the helping professions. But it is one of the most vital rules if we wish to make a space that welcomes soul, the inner teacher.

- *Learn to respond to others with honest, open questions instead of counsel, corrections.* With such questions, we help hear each other into deeper speech.

- *When the going gets rough, turn to wonder.* If you feel judgmental, or defensive, ask yourself, "I wonder what brought her to this belief?" or "I wonder what he's feeling right now?" or "I wonder what my reaction teaches me about myself?" Set aside judgment to listen to others—and to yourself—more deeply.

- *Attend to your own inner teacher.* We learn from others, of course. But as we explore poems, stories, questions, and silence in a circle of trust, we have a special opportunity to learn from within. So pay close attention to your own reactions and responses; to your most important teacher.

- *Trust and learn from the silence.* Silence is a gift in our noisy world, and a way of knowing in itself. Treat silence as a member of the group. After someone has spoken, take time to reflect without immediately filling the space with words.

- *Observe deep confidentiality.* Trust comes from knowing that group members honor confidences and take seriously the ethics of privacy and discretion.

- *Know that it's possible to leave the circle with whatever it was that you needed when you arrived.* Know that the seeds planted here can keep growing in the days ahead.

ACKNOWLEDGEMENTS

THERE ARE SO MANY PEOPLE who have been a part of this endeavor that I wish to thank. I will simply mention their names here without being specific as to why. Sadly, I will have forgotten some significant names that later editions will include. Please forgive me if yours is one of these. My deep gratitude to:

Reverend Gregg Anderson
Rev. Diane Berke
Tessa Bielecki
Bikkhu Bodhi
Reverend Cynthia Bourgeault
Nancy Belle Coe
Katherine and Roger Collis
Father Dave Denny
Lama Palden Drolma
Mollie Favour
Stephanie Glatt
George Haynes
Rabbi Brad Hirschfield
Judy Hyde
Don "Four Arrows" Jacobs
Yogi Nataraja Kallio
Dr. Michael Kearney
Rev. Aaron McEmrys
Sheikh Muhammad Jamal al-Jerrahi (Gregory Blann)
Enrico and Nadia Natali
Susan Pierce

Swami Atmarupananda
John Bennett
Robert Bosnak
Robert Bosnak
Mary Ann Brussat
Sister Brahmaprana
Kathy Corcoran
Laura Dixon
Gordon Dveirin
Rob Gabriel
Dr. John Allen Grimes
Sheikha Camille Helminski
Sister Jose Hobday
Pir Zia Inayat-Khan
Reverend Alan Jones
Father Thomas Keating
Reverend Master Khoten
Robert McDermott
Rabbi Leah Novick
Lexie Potamkin

Reverend Lauren Atress
Rabbi Ozer Bergman
Harvey Bottelsen
Joan Borysenko
Loya Cespooch
Ken Cohen
Anita Daniel
Geshe Lobsang Donyo
Suzanne Farver
Gelek Rinpoche
Roshi Joan Halifax
Sheikh Kabir Helminski
James Hughes
Edie Irons
Chief Oren Lyons
Rabbi Miles Krassen
Acharya Judy Lief
Dena Merriam
Brad Miller
Carol Pearson
Reverend Tenzin Priyadarshi

Margot and Tom Pritzker
Jonathan and Diana Rose
Barbara Sargent
Rabbi Arthur Gross Schaefer
Grace Alvarez Sesma
Ajahn Sona
Michael Stranahan
Geshe Lobsang Tenzin
Pravrajika Vrajaprana
Sharon Wells
Paula Zurcher

Lynda Rae
Rabbi Jeff Roth
Swami Sarvadevananda
Dr. Marilyn Schlitz
Rabbi Rami Shapiro
Geshe Lhundup Sopa
Tekaronianeken Jake Swamp
Juliet Spahn-Twomey
Dr. B. Alan Wallace
Judy Whetstine

Imam Feisal Abdul Rauf
Sharon Salzburg
Rabbi Zalman Schachter-Shalomi
Christiane Schlumberger
Acharya Judith Simmer-Brown
Tina Staley
Brother Wayne Teasdale
Ani Tenzin Kacho
Radhule Weininger
Catherine Wyler

I am also grateful to all those who have studied InterSpiritual Meditation and the Mandala Process Process with me, for they have helped to clarify and refine the ideas and practices described herein. I am indebted to living examples of my mentors and teachers including Geshe Lhundup Sopa, Father Thomas Keating, Rabbi Zalman Schachter, and His Holiness the Dalai Lama. I am grateful to Zachary Malone, Catherine Wyler who helped edit the first edition of this workbook and Lynda Rae for the initial cover design. I am extremely grateful to Juliet Spohn Twomey and La Casa de Maria for providing encouragement and an incubator for this work. My special thanks also to Carol Pearson for her work and mentorship on formation of the Archetypal Spiritual Styles Profile Instruments. I am deeply grateful to the Aspen Chapel for providing a home for Spiritual Paths Foundation and our board of directors including Jay Hughes, Gregg Anderson, Suzanne Farver, John Bennett, Lexie Potamkin, Mike Stranahan and Harvey Bottlesen. And I am infinitely grateful to my family members, Alexandra and Nulty White, Jonathan Bastian, Paul Keeley, Marianne Bastian and to all my ancestors.

Finally, I am grateful to Sam Krezinski for layout design and editing, and to Netanel Miles-Yépez for editing and publishing this book.

ABOUT THE AUTHOR

DR. EDWARD W. BASTIAN holds a Ph.D. in Buddhist Studies and is the founder and president of the Spiritual Paths Foundation. His current writing and teaching is the product of over forty years of research and study, especially in the last decades with over fifty esteemed teachers of Buddhism, Christianity, Hinduism, Islam, Judaism, Taoism, and Native American traditions. He is the award winning co-author of *Living Fully Dying Well* (2009), author of *InterSpiritual Meditation* (2010), and producer of various documentaries on religion for the BBC and PBS.

Bastian is the former co-director of the Forum on BioDiversity for the Smithsonian and National Academy of Sciences, teacher of Buddhism and world religions at the Smithsonian, an Internet entrepreneur and translator of Buddhist scriptures from Tibetan into English. He is also an Adjunct Professor at Antioch University in Santa Barbara where he is teaching courses on Buddhism and Mindfulness Meditation. Bastian also teaches online courses as well as seminars and retreats at such organizations as One Spirit Interfaith, Chaplaincy Institute, CIIS, Sacred Art of Living and Dying, Interspiritual Centre of Vancouver, Cascadia Center, Esalen Institute, Omega Institute, Hollyhock Retreat Center, Garrison Institute and La Casa de Maria.

He is the Co-President of the Interfaith Initiative of Santa Barbara, co-founder of ECOFaith Santa Barbara and Trustee of the United Religions Initiative Global Council.

If you are interested in learning more about retreats, online courses and our mentor training program, please contact me at this email address: ed@spiritualpaths.net

Made in the USA
San Bernardino, CA
16 July 2016